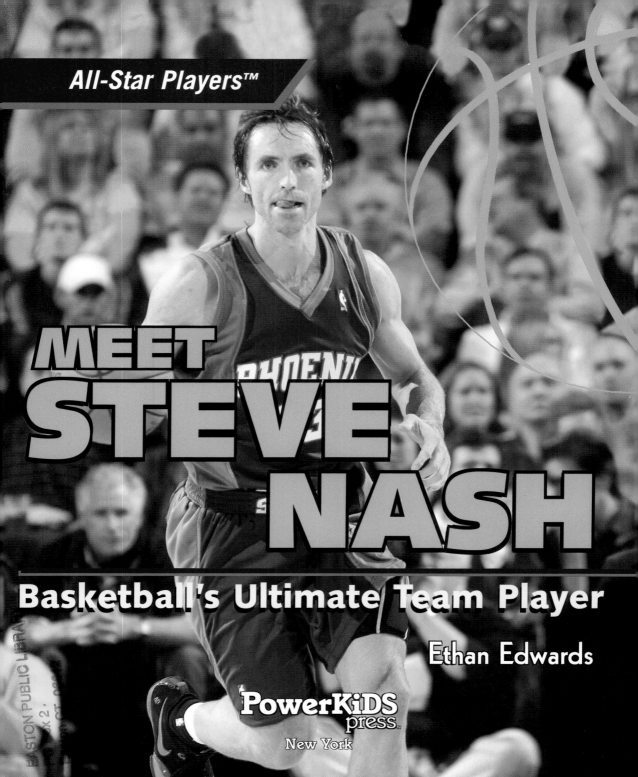

MEET STEVE NASH

Basketball's Ultimate Team Player

Ethan Edwards

PowerKiDS press

New York

Published in 2009 by The Rosen Publishing Group, Inc.
29 East 21st Street, New York, NY 10010

First Edition

Editor: Amelie von Zumbusch
Book Design: Greg Tucker
Photo Researcher: Jessica Gerweck

Photo Credits: Cover, pp. 5, 6, 9, 10, 12, 15, 17, 19, 20, 21, 22, 23, 25, 27, 29, 30 © Getty Images; pp. 13, 26 © NBAE/Getty Images; p. 16 © AFP/Getty Images.

Library of Congress Cataloging-in-Publication Data

Edwards, Ethan.
  Meet Steve Nash : basketball's ultimate team player / Ethan Edwards.
    p. cm. — (All-star players)
  Includes index.
  ISBN 978-1-4042-4489-4 (library binding)
  1. Nash, Steve, 1974– —Juvenile literature. 2. Basketball players—United States—Biography—Juvenile literature. 3. Basketball players—Canada—Biography—Juvenile literature. I. Title.
  GV884.N37E39 2009
  796.323092—dc22
  [B]
                                      2008002120

Manufactured in the United States of America

Contents

Have you ever had a dream or goal? What would you do if someone told you that goal was impossible? If you were like Steve Nash, you would try to reach that goal no matter what anyone said. Basketball coaches and **experts** told Nash that he was too small to play **professional** basketball. Nash is only 6 feet 3 inches (1.9 m) tall. That may sound very tall, but it is small for a player in the NBA, or National Basketball Association.

Nash is now the **point guard** for the Phoenix Suns. However, he is much more than a good point guard. Nash is one of the greatest **athletes** ever to shoot a basketball!

All-Star Facts

In 2006, *Time* magazine ranked Nash as one of the world's 100 most influential people.

Nash (left) worked hard for many years and has now become one of the NBA's top players.

Steve Nash is a Canadian citizen. He played for the Canadian basketball team at the 2000 Olympics.

Soccer, Hockey, Lacrosse, Basketball

Athletic ability runs in the Nash family. Steve's father, John, was a professional soccer player. On February 7, 1974, Steve was born to John and Jean Nash, in the city of Johannesburg, South Africa. Soon after, the family moved to British Columbia, Canada, and Nash grew up there.

Hockey is the national sport of Canada, and Nash and his younger brother, Martin, were excellent hockey players. They also played soccer and lacrosse, but Steve decided that basketball was his favorite sport. When he was in eighth grade, Nash told his mother that he would someday play in the NBA. However, nobody but Nash believed this dream would come true.

All-Star Facts

Steve Nash's full name is Stephen John Nash.

When Nash was in high school, none of the major college basketball **scouts** had heard of him. The only program interested in him was at a small college in California, called Santa Clara University. Santa Clara's head basketball coach flew to Canada to watch Nash play. The coach thought Nash was a great basketball player. He could not believe that nobody else wanted to recruit, or sign up, Nash. The coach offered Nash a full **scholarship** to Santa Clara.

Nash quickly became the star and leader of the Santa Clara Broncos. He was named the West Coast **Conference** Player of the Year two years in a row. He even transformed the losing Broncos into a winning team.

By the time Nash graduated from Santa Clara, he had made more assists and three-point shots than any player in the school's history.

Nash graduated from Santa Clara with a degree in **sociology** in 1996 and decided to try out for the NBA. Basketball teams use a method called a draft to choose young players. Each team takes a turn picking players. The Phoenix Suns chose Nash in the first round of the 1996 NBA Draft. The Suns chose Nash over hundreds of other college athletes. Nash's words to his mother were about to come true.

However, the Suns' fans were disappointed that their team had chosen Nash. Very few people had heard of him. The fans worried that he was too short and skinny to be a good point guard. Unfortunately, Nash did not get much of a chance to prove the fans wrong. The Suns already had

Nash joined the Suns for the 1996–1997 season. However, he got to play an average of only about 10 minutes per game that season.

11

Even though he did not play in as many games as he might have liked, Nash learned a lot playing for the Suns.

two star point guards, named Jason Kidd and Kevin Johnson. Nash learned a lot by watching them play, but he did not get to play very often.

Don Nelson, the head coach of the Dallas Mavericks, had been watching Nash's career.

Nelson knew that though Nash had the **potential** to be a star, he was not getting a chance to prove himself in Phoenix. In 1998, Nelson successfully pushed for Nash to be traded to the Mavericks.

In June 1998, Don Nelson (left) and Steve Nash (right) happily announced that Nash had joined the Mavericks.

In 1998, the Mavericks were not a very good team, and Nash played poorly in his first Dallas season. However, a talented young player named Dirk Nowitzki also joined the Mavericks in 1998. Nash and Nowitzki formed a strong friendship and began playing well together. In 2001, they led the Mavericks to the **play-offs**. Suddenly, Dallas had a good team!

Nash and Nowitzki continued to play well in the 2001–2002 season. Nash was even voted onto the All-Star team. Every year, the very best players at each position compete in the All-Star Game. Nash was one of only 26 players in the entire NBA to be selected.

Nash was often hurt in his early seasons with the Mavericks. In the 2000–2001 season, though, he was healthy and played better than he ever had before.

Nash (left) and Nowitzki (right) helped make the Mavericks one of the NBA's strongest teams.

The Mavericks opened the 2002–2003 season by winning 14 games in a row. Dallas became an **elite** team, and Nash and Nowitzki became superstars. However, in 2004, the Mavericks' management decided that the team needed only one superstar. They decided to build a young team around Nowitzki. This meant they would have to trade Nash to another team. Nash did not want to leave the Mavericks. He would miss Nowitzki. Many teams were interested in Nash, but the Suns jumped at the chance to bring him back to Phoenix. This time, the fans did not complain!

Nash continued to play well in the 2003–2004 season, his final season with the Mavericks.

The Suns had finished the 2003–2004 season with a horrible record. They had talented players, but they needed a leader. When Nash joined the team in July 2004, he stepped into that role, or part, and turned the team around. The Suns finished the 2004–2005 regular season with the best record in the NBA. Once again, Nash had helped turn one of the worst teams into one of the best.

Nash became known for his ability to make assists. Assists happen when a player helps a teammate score by passing that teammate the ball. Assists require teamwork. Nash is excellent at finding open teammates down the court. Good

After he returned to the Suns, Steve Nash continued to wear the number 13, as he had throughout his time in the NBA.

In the 2004–2005 season, Nash had a higher average number of assists than any NBA player had had in the last 10 years.

point guards know when to pass the ball to the right player. Nash is a great point guard. If Nash cannot make a shot himself, he will always pass to the teammate who can. This makes him a dangerous **opponent** when he has the ball.

The Most Valuable Player

Nash played so well in the 2004–2005 season that he was voted MVP by America's basketball **journalists**. "MVP" means "most valuable player." Only one player in the entire NBA wins this award each year. The MVP award is basketball's highest honor for a single player. Nash became the first Canadian ever to win the award. Nash also became the third point guard to be named the MVP.

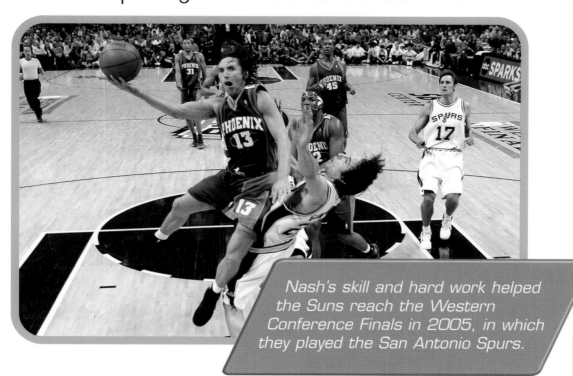

Nash's skill and hard work helped the Suns reach the Western Conference Finals in 2005, in which they played the San Antonio Spurs.

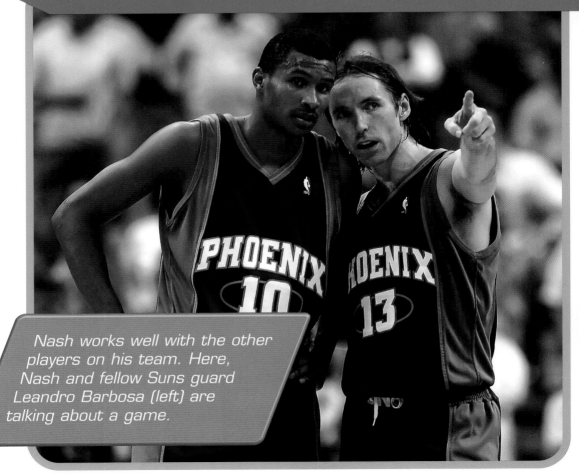

Nash works well with the other players on his team. Here, Nash and fellow Suns guard Leandro Barbosa (left) are talking about a game.

Nash played his best basketball yet in the 2005–2006 season. He led the league in assists, and the Suns scored more points than any other team in the NBA. Nash made basketball history at the end of the season by winning the MVP for a second year in a row! Fewer than a dozen other basketball players have ever been named the MVP more than once. So much for being too small to play basketball!

Nash (right) is only the ninth player in the history of the NBA to be named MVP two years in a row.

Nash is busy off the court, too. He and his wife, Alejandra Amarilla, have twin daughters, called Lola and Bella. Dirk Nowitzki is the girls' godfather.

Nash is still a big soccer fan. His brother and many of his friends play professional soccer. Nash and Dirk Nowitzki often attend soccer games together. Nash also loves to read. One of his favorite authors is a **philosopher** named Immanuel Kant. Nash is interested in **politics**, too. At the 2003 All-Star Game, he protested the Iraq War by wearing a T-shirt that said, "No War. Shoot for Peace." His T-shirt created a big **controversy**.

All-Star Facts

In 2005, *GQ* magazine named Steve Nash to its best-dressed list.

Alejandra Amarilla (left) and Steve Nash (right) were married in June 2005. Amarilla is from the South American country of Paraguay.

Both of Nash's daughters are known by nicknames. Lola (left) is short for Lourdes, and Bella (middle) is short for Isabella.

Nash is also active with several **charities**. He knows that he can use his fame and money to help others. In 2001, he created the Steve Nash Foundation to raise money to improve the health and education of children from poor families. Nash considers his two homes to be Phoenix, Arizona, and British Columbia, Canada. Therefore, the Steve

Nash Foundation helps children in Phoenix and British Columbia.

Nash has also joined a Canadian organization called Gulu Walk. Gulu Walk raises money to help children affected by war and **poverty** in the African country of Uganda. Nash bought expensive medical **equipment** for a hospital in the South American country of Paraguay, too.

In 2007, Nash (right) and fellow NBA player Yao Ming (left) hosted the Yao-Nash Gala to raise money for schools in poor parts of western China.

Nash continues to play astonishing basketball. He led the NBA in assists for three seasons in a row, between 2004 and 2007. In 2007, he nearly won a third MVP award but came in second place to Dirk Nowitzki. That same year, the journalists at ESPN ranked Nash as the ninth-best point guard of all time!

The people who said Nash was too small to play basketball were obviously wrong. It is a good thing he did not listen to them. Instead, Nash has become one of the greatest basketball players ever. Think of him the next time you hear somebody say, "That's impossible!"

All-Star Facts

Nash is the third-best free-throw shooter of all time. He is also the sixth-best three-point shooter of all time!

Nash's many years of hard work have paid off. He is now one of the very best players in the NBA.

Height: 6' 3" (1.9 m)
Weight: 178 pounds (81 kg)
Team: Phoenix Suns
Position: Point guard
Uniform Number: 13
Date of Birth: February 7, 1974

2006–2007 Season Stats

Games Played	3-Point Percentage	Free-Throw Percentage	Rebounds per Game	Assists per Game	Points per Game
76	.455	.899	3.5	11.6	18.6

NBA Career Stats as of Summer 2007

Games Played	3-Point Percentage	Free-Throw Percentage	Rebounds per Game	Assists per Game	Points per Game
779	.42	.88	2.85	7.33	13.41

Glossary

athletes (ATH-leets) People who take part in sports.

charities (CHER-uh-teez) Groups that give help to the needy.

conference (KON-frens) A grouping of sports teams.

controversy (KON-truh-ver-see) Something that causes disagreement.

elite (ay-LEET) Part of a small, powerful group.

equipment (uh-KWIP-mint) All the supplies needed to do an activity.

experts (EK-sperts) People who know a lot about a subject.

journalists (JER-nul-ists) People who gather and write news for newspapers or magazines.

opponent (uh-POH-nent) A person or a group that is against another.

philosopher (fih-LAH-suh-fer) A person who tries to discover and to understand the basic nature of knowledge.

play-offs (PLAY-ofs) Games played after the regular season ends to see who will play in the championship game.

point guard (POYNT GAHRD) A basketball player who directs his or her team's forward plays on the court.

politics (PAH-lih-tiks) The science of governments and elections.

potential (poh-TEN-shul) Promise.

poverty (PAH-ver-tee) The state of being poor.

professional (pruh-FESH-nul) Someone who is paid for what he or she does.

scholarship (SKAH-lur-ship) Money given to someone to pay for school.

scouts (SKOWTS) People who help sports teams find new, young players.

sociology (soh-see-O-luh-jee) The study of human societies and social activities.

Index

Web Sites

Due to the changing nature of Internet links, PowerKids Press
has developed an online list of Web sites related to the subject
of this book. This site is updated regularly. Please use this link to
access the list:
www.powerkidslinks.com/asp/nash/